CHI

3/07

D1486882

How to Draw the Life and Times of
Zachary Taylor

Roderic Schmidt

The Rosen Publishing Group's
PowerKids Press™
New York

To my father

Published in 2006 by The Rosen Publishing Group, Inc.
29 East 21st Street, New York, NY 10010

First Edition

Editors: Melissa Acevedo and Orli Zuravicky
Layout Design: Julio A. Gil

Illustrations: All illustrations by Albert Hanner
Photo Credits: p. 4 © Atwater Kent Museum of Philadelphia/Bridgeman Art Library/Courtesy of Historical Society of Pennsylvania Collection; p. 7 © Bettmann/Corbis; pp. 8 (left), 9 © Benton J. Nelson, www.presidentsgraves.com; pp. 10, 12, 14, 26 Library of Congress Prints and Photographs Division; p. 16 Wisconsin Historical Society, Image ID: 25581; p. 18 © North Wind Picture Archives; p. 22 Courtesy of Dr. Benjamin Weiss, Ph.D., historicalartmedals.com; pp. 24, 28 Picture History.

Library of Congress Cataloging-in-Publication Data

Schmidt, Roderic.
How to draw the life and times of Zachary Taylor / Roderic Schmidt.
    p. cm. — (A kid's guide to drawing the presidents of the United States of America)
Includes bibliographical references and index.
ISBN 1-4042-2989-2 (library binding)
1. Taylor, Zachary, 1784–1850—Juvenile literature. 2. Presidents—United States—Biography—Juvenile literature. 3. Drawing—Technique—Juvenile literature. I. Title. II. Series.

E422.S36 2006
973.6'3'092—dc22

                          2004019480

Manufactured in the United States of America

Contents

Life Before Politics

Zachary Taylor was a courageous soldier and the twelfth president of the United States. He was born in Orange County, Virginia, on November 24, 1784. His father, Richard Taylor, had served in the Continental army during the American Revolution. As a reward  for his service in the Revolution, he was given a plot of land near Louisville, Kentucky. Right after Taylor was born, his family moved to Kentucky and began a new life on the western frontier. At this time much of the western frontier was still wilderness. Sometimes Taylor could hear wolves howling at night and the Native Americans and settlers fighting nearby.

Young Taylor was briefly educated by a private tutor, but he spent most of his time learning about farming. He helped his father build and run their plantation. At the age of 23, Taylor joined the U.S. Army. He was a commander of forts and a field officer in the army from 1808 to 1848. In 1846,

America fought against Mexico in the Mexican War. America won in 1848. Zachary Taylor became a national hero because of all the battles he won while fighting this war. With such an excellent leadership record, many people thought that he would make a good president and convinced him to run. Before running for president, Taylor had to decide which political party he wanted to join. He realized that he agreed most with the Whig Party, whose main concerns were improving businesses and fixing the roads and canals of America. Taylor ran for president in 1848 as the Whig candidate.

You will need the following supplies to draw the life and times of Zachary Taylor:

✓ A sketch pad   ✓ An eraser   ✓ A pencil   ✓ A ruler

These are some of the shapes and drawing terms you need to know:

Horizontal Line	——	Squiggly Line	∿
Oval	⬭	Trapezoid	⏢
Rectangle	▭	Triangle	△
Shading	▰	Vertical Line	│
Slanted Line	/	Wavy Line	⌒

The Short Presidency of Zachary Taylor

Slavery was an important issue in the 1848 election. Zachary Taylor owned slaves but opposed the spread of slavery. He believed slavery was only necessary to run a cotton plantation, and therefore he was against the spread of slavery in areas where cotton could not grow. Northerners saw Taylor as committed to keeping the country united. Southerners saw Taylor as a plantation owner who understood their need for slavery. Since he was able to appeal to both sides, Zachary Taylor won the election.

The issue of slavery was a major problem for Taylor. Northern and southern states could not agree on whether slavery should be allowed in the new land America gained in the Mexican War. Taylor also had to decide how large each new territory would be. He dealt with border disagreements between the new territories, which included Texas and New Mexico. Sadly Taylor died after only 16 months in office. Many of the problems he worked on while in office were not solved until after his death.

Based on a quick drawing done on the spot by William Croome, this print was created by Brightly and Keyster. The drawing shows Taylor on the steps of the Capitol during his swearing in on March 5, 1849.

Zachary Taylor's Kentucky

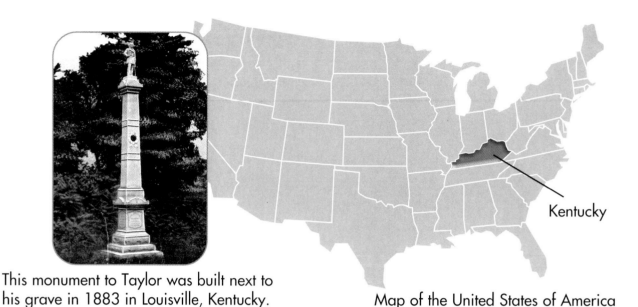

This monument to Taylor was built next to his grave in 1883 in Louisville, Kentucky.

Map of the United States of America

Kentucky

When Zachary Taylor was growing up in Kentucky, it had not yet become a state. When it finally became a state in 1792, Kentucky was not heavily populated. The Taylors' farm, Springfield, was located about 5 miles (8 km) from Louisville, Kentucky, near the Ohio River. Louisville's population was small. In 1800, there were only 359 people living in Louisville. Bad roads made traveling to Louisville hard, and the Native Americans who lived nearby were not always friendly. However, as time passed, the city became more popular. It also became wealthy because of the successful trade of goods along the Ohio River. By 1810, Louisville had homes that were as beautiful as those found in established cities, such as Philadelphia or New York City. Louisville's wealthy occupants threw fancy parties and wore the most current fashions.

When Taylor died in 1850, his body was brought from Washington, D.C., the capital of the United States, to Louisville, Kentucky, to be buried. In 1883, the U.S. Senate had a monument, which was topped by a statue of Zachary Taylor, built next to his grave. The cemetery where Taylor is buried is now called the Zachary Taylor National Cemetery. It is located in Jefferson County, a county in Louisville, Kentucky. The cemetery belongs to the Taylor family, and most of the people buried there are members of Taylor's family.

The above picture shows the front of the grave of Zachary Taylor. Every year on November 24, Taylor's birth date, soldiers have a wreath-laying ceremony in front of his grave.

A Career in the Army

The military was important to the Taylor family. Zachary Taylor's father, Richard, had fought in the American Revolution. His older brother, William, had also joined the

army. In 1808, Taylor decided to follow in the family's footsteps and he signed up for the army.

Taylor's first appointment was first lieutenant, which meant he was an officer in charge of a small number of soldiers. It is said that his distant cousin James Madison, who was president at the time, arranged for Taylor to begin his military career with an officer's ranking. Taylor always made sure that his soldiers were busy, even when they were not fighting. He became known for maintaining control over his soldiers. In 1810, Taylor was promoted to captain. His work in the army required travel, but he visited his home, shown above, in Louisville whenever he could. Taylor married Margaret Mackall Smith in 1810. During their happy marriage, they raised four children.

1

Zachary Taylor's house is located in Jefferson County, Kentucky, and it is considered to be a historic building. Begin the house by drawing a large rectangle as a guide.

2

Use a square to form the outline for the front of the house. Use straight lines for the sides and draw the roof. Add a vertical line coming out from the roof on the right side.

3

Draw the porch on the right side. Begin by making the roof and the base. To draw the rails, add vertical lines as shown. The rails connect to the top and bottom of the porch as shown.

4

Outline the edge of the house and porch using straight lines. Draw vertical lines on the porch rails. Draw horizontal lines between the rails. Erase any extra lines.

5

Using rectangles, add windows to the front and side of the house as shown. Draw two vertical lines to create the doorway of the front porch. Using horizontal lines, add stairs to the porch.

6

Draw three chimneys on the roof of the house. Add lines to the windows for details and a long vertical line to the left side of the house for the drain pipe. At the base of the house, add bushes.

7

Erase the rectangular guide and extra lines. Add shapes to the windows. Add lines to the base of the house, the door and the chimneys. Add slanted horizontal lines as shown for the ground.

8

Finish your drawing by shading in the house as shown. Notice that the shading is darker in some spots than in others. Great work!

Soldier in the War of 1812

The War of 1812 was Zachary Taylor's first major war. America went to war against England to protect their ships from English attacks. At this time, Taylor  was commanding Fort Harrison, shown above, in the Indiana Territory. The nearby Native Americans were led by a man named Chief Tecumseh. He was on the side of the English because they offered to help him get Native American land back from American settlers. Taylor feared Tecumseh would attack Fort Harrison, so he had his army of about 55 men repair the fort.

As Taylor had feared, in September of 1812, a group of about 450 Native Americans attacked Fort Harrison. The Native Americans set the fort on fire, but Taylor had his men drive the Native Americans away from the fort. Although this was Taylor's first battle and his force was outnumbered, he remained calm. By not panicking, Taylor was able to command his men well under trying conditions and win the battle.

1

The drawing of Fort Harrison was created in 1812. To draw the fort, begin by drawing a large rectangle. This will be your guide.

2

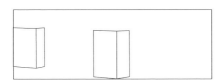

Inside the rectangular guide, draw four vertical, slightly slanted rectangles as shown. These rectangles will be part of the front of the fort.

3

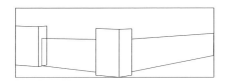

Draw two horizontal lines connecting the rectangles from step 2. Then draw a vertical line connecting the two horizontal lines you just drew. Draw a slanting rectangle on the right side as shown.

4

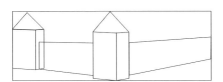

Add two triangles on top of the rectangles from step 1.

5

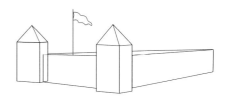

Erase the rectangular guide from step 1. Add lines across the back of the fort as shown. Add slanted vertical lines to the triangles. Add a line for the flag pole and draw the flag as shown.

6

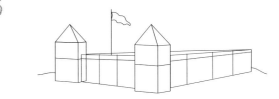

Add lines to the sides of the fort. The lines should connect as shown above. Add a horizontal line to each rectangle from step 2. Add a slanted line to the bottom of the left and right sides of the fort for the ground.

7

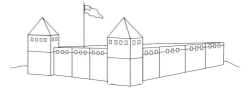

Erase any extra lines. Draw small rectangles for the windows of the fort as shown. When drawing them, make sure there is enough space between each window. Add a small shape to the upper left corner of the flag.

8

Finish your drawing of Fort Harrison with shading. Be sure to shade the flag so that it looks like it has stripes. Good job!

Fighting the Black Hawk War

After the War of 1812 ended, Zachary Taylor commanded forts all over the western United States. In 1832, he was promoted to colonel and given control of Fort Crawford in the Wisconsin Territory. Not long after Taylor's promotion, the Black Hawk War broke out between America and a group of Sauk Native Americans.

The Black Hawk War started when the leader of the Sauk tribe, Chief Black Hawk, decided that America should return the land that it had taken away from the Sauks. He led his followers east from the Iowa Territory toward Illinois. The U.S. Army sent troops, including Taylor and his men, to search for the tribe. Realizing he did not have enough men for a fight, Black Hawk led his group back west. The U.S. Army found them and in August 1832, they fought the major battle of the war on the banks of the Bad Axe River. Black Hawk and his group were defeated. At the end of the war, Taylor and his men returned to Fort Crawford.

1

The painting of Black Hawk was created by McKenney & Hall in 1838. Begin by drawing a large guide rectangle.

2

Inside the rectangle, draw two ovals that overlap. These ovals will be the guides for the head and neck of Black Hawk.

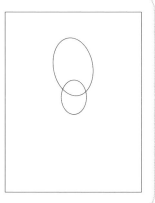

3

In the larger oval, draw a horizontal line that extends outside the oval on both sides. Next draw a curved vertical line that extends through both ovals. These two lines must cross.

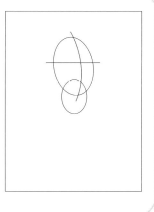

4

Draw the shape on the top oval as shown. This is the guide for the headdress. Draw two curved lines from the first oval to the base of the rectangle for the body.

5

Using the intersected lines in the oval, draw the eyes, eyebrows, nose, mouth, and ears. Use a curved line to add shape to the face as shown. Using curved lines, draw the shirt collar and neck.

6

Erase extra lines. Use lines to add the band and the feathers to the headdress. Add curved lines to the inside of the ears. Add lines to the body for the cloth. Add the medal as shown.

7

Erase any extra lines. Add earrings to the ears. Add lines to the face, eyes, and neck for wrinkles and details. Add the beads around his neck. Add more lines to his clothing.

8

Finish the drawing of Black Hawk by shading in the figure. Notice that some parts of the drawing are darker than other parts. Excellent work!

Officer and Father

Early on in Zachary Taylor's army career, he was required to move around a lot. He lived at Fort Crawford, shown in  the picture on the right, until 1837. At Fort Crawford, Taylor's wife, Margaret, and their four children were all able to live with him. The Taylors enjoyed life at Fort Crawford. Officers held dances and parties for one another. Two of Taylor's daughters, Ann and Sarah, married officers they met at Fort Crawford.

Taylor made the fort as comfortable as possible for the men living there. Merchants had settled near Fort Crawford and sold all types of things to the soldiers. The fort had a library and a school for the soldiers' children. The soldiers would sometimes change their rooms into theaters and put on plays. Taylor and his family would often invite people to dine at their home. Their guests were always pleased by the pleasantness of the family. Taylor's time at Fort Crawford was a special one for him and his family.

1

This illustration of Fort Crawford was created in 1830. Fort Crawford, named for William H. Crawford, secretary of war at the time, was built in Mississippi in 1816. To draw the fort, begin with a long rectangle.

2

Add another long shape. Draw two smaller shapes connecting to the larger one on the right side. Draw the triangular shape on the left side of the large rectangle as shown.

3

On top of the shapes you just drew in step 2, draw the roof shapes as shown. Use triangles and straight lines.

4

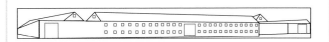

Add small squares for windows to the front of the fort and to the roof. Draw three big doors on the fort.

5

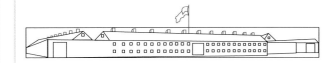

Add small chimneys to the roof. Add a vertical line to the roof for the flagpole. Draw a squiggly shape for the flag, so it looks like the flag is waving. Add a shape to the corner of the flag. This shape is called the canton.

6

Erase the rectangular guide. Finish your drawing by shading. Notice how some parts of the fort are darker than others. Your fort looks wonderful!

The Second Seminole War

In 1835, the government wanted the Native American Seminole nation to move west from their homeland in Florida to what is now

Oklahoma in order to build on their land. The Seminoles refused to leave and the Second Seminole War began. In 1837, Zachary Taylor went to the Florida Territory to command troops. The army was ordered to remove the Seminoles from the area. This was not easy because the Seminole people knew their land well and hid from the soldiers.

In December 1837, Taylor and his men defeated Seminole warriors at the Battle of Okeechobee. Taylor was promoted to brigadier general, and most of the Seminole nation was forced to move west. It was during this war that Taylor earned the nickname "Old Rough and Ready" because he was willing to live in the same rough conditions as his soldiers did. In 1840, Taylor left Florida, at his own request, and was relocated to Louisiana. The painting above shows two Seminoles in a canoe.

1

This hand-colored woodcut created in the 1800s shows two Seminole Native Americans in a dugout canoe. The canoe is made from a cypress log. To draw this picture, start with a large rectangle.

2

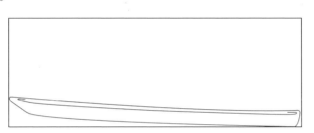

At the base of the rectangle, draw a slanted canoe. Be sure to note that the left side of the canoe is slightly pointed and is higher up than the right side. Then draw a curved line on the inside of the shape as shown.

3

Erase the rectangle. Draw the outline of two people in the boat as shown. One person should be standing and the other person should be sitting. These will be the outlines for the Seminole Native Americans in the canoe.

4

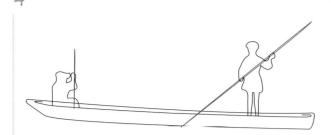

Draw a vertical line in the hands of the Seminole sitting on the left side of the canoe. Draw a slanted line in the hands of the Seminole standing on the right side. This is a pole.

5

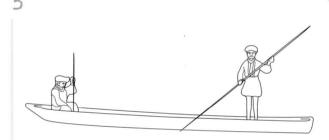

Erase the lines of the boat that pass through the figures. Add faces to the two Seminoles. Add the clothing and hands to each figure as shown.

6

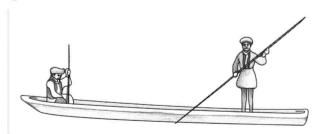

Add a slightly curved line that goes across the top of the canoe. Finish the drawing by shading. Notice which parts of the Seminoles' clothes are darker. Good job!

Beginnings of Fame and the Mexican War

In 1840, Zachary Taylor bought a plantation in Louisiana. He spent the next five years managing it and commanding forts along the Mississippi River. In 1845, Texas and Mexico began arguing about the location of the border they shared. Texas wanted the border to lie south of the Rio Grande, while Mexico wanted the border to be north.

In January 1846, Taylor and his troops were sent to the Rio Grande to guard Texas from Mexican troops. In May 1846, the Mexican army crossed the Rio Grande. Taylor and his men forced the Mexican soldiers back. On May 8 and 9, Taylor defeated larger Mexican forces at the battles at Palo Alto and Resaca de la Palma. He was promoted to major general. The Mexican War had begun.

In 1847, some American officers in Mexico City decided to form a social club, which they called the Aztec Club of 1847. The club's crest is shown above. Taylor and other future president Franklin Pierce joined.

1

To draw the crest of the Aztec Club of 1847, start with a large circle.

2

Inside the large circle, draw a smaller circle.

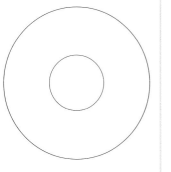

3

Inside the smaller circle, draw the shape of an eagle. Be sure to include the beak and the two feet.

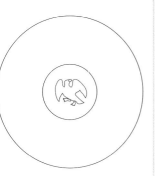

4

Add an eye and a snake in the mouth of the eagle. Draw four shapes that come out of the small circle as shown. In between each of the four shapes, add three shapes as shown.

5

Erase the lines of the eagle that go through the snake. Inside the four big shapes, draw two of the same shapes, only smaller. Inside the smaller shapes, draw only one of the same shape.

6

Inside the smaller shapes, draw lines that slant toward the center. Look at the picture carefully while adding these lines.

7

Add in the text that is in the inner circle. The text that should go above the eagle is "CITY OF MEXICO." The text that should go on the bottom of the circle is "ARMY OF OCCUPATION."

8

Finish the drawing of the Aztec Club crest by shading. Be sure to note that some parts of the drawing are shaded darker than others. Great job!

From the Battle of Buena Vista to Presidential Nominee

After defeating the Mexican army in May 1846, Zachary Taylor was given the job of attacking Mexico and taking over some of its land. Taylor left Texas with about 7,000 men in the summer of 1846. In  late September, they entered the city of Monterrey. After three days of fighting the Mexican troops, Taylor won. In January 1847, the U.S. Army took Taylor's best soldiers to fight in other areas of Mexico. He was left with just 5,000 men. General Santa Anna, the commander of the Mexican army, found out about Taylor's loss of men and in February 1847, he and 20,000 Mexican soldiers attacked Taylor's force at Buena Vista. Under Taylor's skillful command, the Mexican army was defeated. The medal shown above celebrates Taylor's victory. Americans began thinking that he would make a good president. People formed "Old Rough and Ready" clubs and worked to drum up support for Taylor's nomination.

1

The bronze medal celebrating Taylor's Mexican War victory was created by Charles Cushing Wright in 1848. The medal shows the battle at Buena Vista. Begin by drawing a circle.

2

Draw another circle inside the circle from step 1. Make this circle a little smaller.

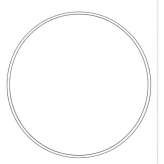

3

Draw two more circles inside the circle you just made in step 2. Make each one a little smaller than the last one.

4

Add the text to the top of the circle. The text you will add is "BUENA VISTA FEB. 22. & 23. 1847."

5

Using curved lines, draw two snakes that cross at their heads and their tails. Use the picture as a guide for how they are supposed to look. They should form a circle.

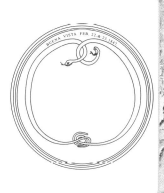

6

Using lines, draw in mountains below the snakes' heads as shown. Then draw in leaves with branches under the snakes' connected tails. Pay close attention to the picture to add detail.

7

Draw the figures on horseback as shown. Draw the soldiers using lines that are close together. Add in the hills and the other details on the medal. This step is hard, so work slowly.

8

Finish your drawing by shading. Look at the medal and note how some places are darker than others. Excellent work!

President of the People

America won the Mexican War in 1848, and gained the land that is now Arizona, California, Nevada, New Mexico, Utah, and Colorado.  In June 1848, Zachary Taylor accepted the Whig Party nomination. The poster shown here is from his campaign. After winning the election, he left the army in January 1849. President Taylor's first important decision was how to deal with slavery in the territory America got from the Mexican War. Southern states wanted the territories to allow slavery, while northern states did not. Taylor advised both California and New Mexico to apply for statehood. Then each would have the right to decide whether it would be a free state or a slave state. If they remained territories, Congress would have the power to decide whether they would allow slavery or not. Taylor thought that statehood was the best opportunity for peace. However, southern congressmen knew that New Mexico and California would apply as free states and refused to grant them statehood.

1

The eagle was taken from the top of a Zachary Taylor campaign poster created in 1846. To begin drawing the eagle, start with a large rectangle.

2

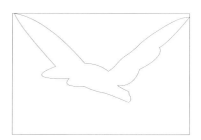

Inside the rectangle draw the outline of the eagle as shown.

3

Using lines, add the feathers to the wings of the eagle as shown. Add shapes to the top of the eagle's back as shown. These are more feathers.

4

Draw in the eye and beak of the eagle as shown. Add in lines to the bottom of the eagle for the feathers. Draw the claws of the eagle. Make sure the left claw looks like it is holding onto an object as shown.

5

Draw zigzag lines coming out of the object that is in the eagle's left claw. Add details to the claws. Add lines to the eye and beak of the eagle as shown.

6

Erase the rectangle you drew in step 1 and all the body guides. Finish the drawing by shading. Add some upside-down *U*'s on the wings for feathers. Great work!

President Taylor and the Slavery Issue

In January 1850, Congressman Henry Clay introduced a bill called the Compromise of 1850. To satisfy the northern states, the compromise allowed California to become a free state and ended slavery in Washington, D.C. It also stopped the expansion of the slave state of

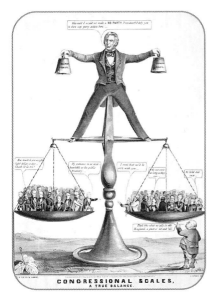

Texas by deciding on the location of a border. To satisfy the southerners, the compromise let the other new territories decide the slavery issue for themselves. It also created the Fugitive Slave Law, which required the return of runaway slaves to their owners. Clay thought the compromise would calm the North and the South. However, Zachary Taylor opposed the bill. He agreed with many parts of the bill, but he felt that each issue should be dealt with individually. On July 9, 1850, Taylor died of an illness while Congress was still deciding on the compromise. After Taylor's death the parts of the compromise were divided into separate bills, just as he had wished. Each bill passed.

1

The political cartoon on page 26 shows Taylor trying to keep the balance between the North and South about slavery. It was created by N. Currier in 1850. Draw a large vertical rectangle.

2

Draw two lines that extend past the lines of the rectangle from step 1. Draw one vertical and one horizontal line and make sure they cross.

3

Draw a long oval along the vertical line and a rectangle around the horizontal lines. Draw three triangular shapes at the bottom of the rectangle. They will have a round bottom.

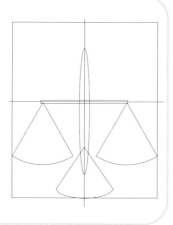

4

Erase the horizontal and vertical lines. Draw in the guide ovals for the figure that will be at the top of the scale. Add two squares hanging down from the horizontal oval.

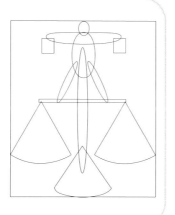

5

In the bottom triangular shape, use curved lines to make the scale's base. Add the shapes in the other two triangular shapes as shown. Add the details to the scale using lines as shown.

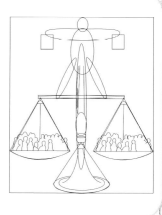

6

Add a face and hair to the figure. Using lines, add his clothes, including a little bow tie. Using curved lines, make the squares look like bells or weights.

7

Erase the guides from the drawing. Add details to President Taylor's clothes and to the weights. Add details to the horizontal pole on which he is standing.

8

Finish the drawing by shading. If you want, you can continue your drawing by looking at the picture on page 26 and adding the rest. Great work!

Old Rough and Ready

Zachary Taylor was a man who spent his whole life serving the United States, a country that he loved dearly. He was a brave man who was well liked and respected by his soldiers. He was both a popular war hero and president. Throughout Taylor's

career he always acted in the way that he felt was best for the country.

Even though Taylor's presidency was short, he understood that the country was struggling with the issue of slavery. He tried to prevent the struggle from tearing the country apart. Even though he owned slaves, he knew that if slavery was allowed to expand, it could be the cause of a civil war.

Zachary Taylor was a man committed to his country. He was always ready to perform his duty for America and was unafraid of any suffering that may have come his way. He truly was "Old Rough and Ready."

1

The painting on page 28 of Zachary Taylor was created by James Reid Lambdin in 1848. Start your drawing of the painting by making a large rectangle.

2

Add an oval near the top of the rectangle. This will be the guide for Taylor's head. Next draw the guide shape for his body using curved lines. Be sure to include the curve for the collar.

3

Using squiggly lines, draw in Taylor's hair on the oval. Using curved lines, outline the guides you made for the face and body to give Taylor more detail.

4

Erase the guides from step 2. Draw the eyes, nose, eyebrows, and mouth. Add in the ear on the right side.

5

Using lines, add Taylor's collar. Add more lines to his coat as shown. Be sure to include the rough vertical line for his sleeve.

6

Add lines to Taylor's face for wrinkles. Add lines to the ears and hair. Add lines to the jacket for details.

7

Add more lines to the face and ear as shown. Add circles and ovals to the jacket for buttons. Add more lines to the jacket to show folds.

8

Finish your drawing of President Taylor by shading him in. Wonderful job!

Timeline

1784 Zachary Taylor is born on November 24 in Virginia.

1792 Kentucky, Taylor's home state, finally becomes a state.

1808 Taylor joins the U.S. Army at the age of 23. His first appointment is as a first lieutenant.

1810 Thanks to his hard work and control over his soldiers, Zachary Taylor is promoted to captain.

Taylor marries Margaret Mackall Smith.

1812 America goes to war against England in the War of 1812.

In September 1812, Taylor defeats a group of Native Americans who attack Fort Harrison.

1832 Zachary Taylor is promoted to colonel and is given control of Fort Crawford in the Wisconsin Territory.

Taylor fights in the Black Hawk War in a battle on the banks of the Bad Axe River.

1837 Taylor leaves Fort Crawford to go to the Florida Territory to fight in the Second Seminole War.

He defeats the Seminole warriors in the Battle of Okeechobee. He earns the nickname "Old Rough and Ready."

1840 At his own request, Taylor is relocated from Florida to Louisiana. He then buys a plantation in Louisiana.

1846 Taylor is sent to the Rio Grande to guard Texas from Mexican troops. His army defeats Mexican troops in the battles of Palo Alto and Resaca de la Palma.

Taylor is promoted to major general.

1847 Taylor joins the Aztec Club of 1847.

1848 Zachary Taylor runs for president as the Whig Party candidate.

1849 Taylor wins the election and becomes the twelfth U.S. president.

1850 Zachary Taylor dies suddenly on July 9 while Congress is still deciding on the Compromise of 1850.

Glossary

American Revolution (uh-MER-uh-ken reh-vuh-LOO-shun) Battles that soldiers from the colonies fought against Britain for freedom, from 1775 to 1783.

bill (BIL) A suggested law presented to the government for approval.

candidate (KAN-dih-dayt) A person who runs in an election.

cemetery (SEH-muh-ter-ee) A place where the dead are buried.

civil war (SIH-vul WOR) A war between two sides within one country.

compromise (KOM-pruh-myz) An agreement in which both sides give up something.

Continental army (kon-ti-NEN-tul AR-mee) The army of patriots created in 1775, with George Washington as its commander in chief.

defeated (dih-FEET-ed) Bested in a contest or battle.

expansion (ek-SPAN-shun) The widening or opening of an area.

frontier (frun-TEER) The edge of a settled country, where the wilderness begins.

Indiana Territory (in-dee-A-nuh TEHR-uh-tor-ee) An area of land, which has become the present-day states of Illinois, Wisconsin, most of Indiana, the eastern part of Minnesota, and the western half of Michigan.

medal (MEH-dul) A small, round piece of metal that is given as a prize.

nomination (nah-mih-NAY-shun) The suggestion that someone or something should be given an award or a position.

plantation (plan-TAY-shun) A very large farm where crops are grown.

political party (puh-LIH-tih-kul PAR-tee) A group of people who have similar beliefs in how the government affairs should be run.

promoted (pruh-MOHT-ed) To be raised in rank or importance.

statue (STA-chyoo) An image of a person or an animal, usually cut in clay, metal, or stone.

territory (TER-uh-tor-ee) Land that is controlled by a person or a group of people.

tutor (TOO-ter) Someone who teaches one student or a small group of students.

united (yoo-NYT-ed) Brought together to act as a single group.

Whig Party (WIG PAR-tee) A political party formed in 1834.

Index

Web Sites

Due to the changing nature of Internet links, PowerKids Press has developed an online list of Web sites related to the subject of this book. This site is updated regularly. Please use this link to access the list:
www.powerkidslinks.com/kgdpusa/taylor/